Through the Years

A Book of Poems

Princess Worrell

authorHOUSE®

AuthorHouse™
1663 Liberty Drive
Bloomington, IN 47403
www.authorhouse.com
Phone: 1 (800) 839-8640

Published by AuthorHouse   04/01/2015

ISBN: 978-1-5049-0428-5 (sc)
ISBN: 978-1-5049-0425-4 (e)

Print information available on the last page.

Any people depicted in stock imagery provided by Thinkstock are models,
and such images are being used for illustrative purposes only.
Certain stock imagery © Thinkstock.

This book is printed on acid-free paper.

I dedicate this book to my mom and dad and my brothers and sister in heaven. To my sisters and brothers and family and friends who have been there thank you and I love you. To my children James, Whitney, and Tiffany I love you. To you who inspired me thank you I love you too, loving someone through life is a beautiful thing and never letting go of that special joy that one brings.

Still in love

Tell me why am I chasing an empty rainbow if there's no pot of gold at the other end
broken hopes and dreams with no future in it
So many tears shed so little strength left just trying to stay ahead
So many set backs still and all just trying to give it my best
and not even returned a little bit like I gave it
Hearts sometimes break if you're not careful of what you do or say
and picking up the pieces isn't a easy task no matter how many times it breaks
So scared of breaking so your mind tells you not to fall too deep like walking a tight rope
you're scared of falling so you try to creep
But my mind never told my heart the game and no one tells you when you're young that
falling in love could be so dangerous it's like a time bomb ready to explode set a time and
your heart will be gone
And when that happens you'll still be in love

Perfect

I always dreamed love to be so perfect but it's not

It has so many ups and downs so much confusion

But when it's good its really good you can feel all it's love and more

You flow with so much energy so much feeling your so high

You believe you can do anything that you want

Love isn't suppose to hurt you're suppose to feel joy with love

But that's not always the case love is whatever you make it

In love

Tell me only this that I have your heart for always

And you want me by your side whispering the words I will always love you

And forever I will be your lover and I know if you really care you will always be there

Now I need to tell you this there's no other love like your love

And as long as I live I will give you all the joy my heart and soul can give

So let me hold you I need to have you near me and feel you in my arms

This love will last forever cause I'm truly in love with you and I'm head over heels in love

I wonder

I wonder what it feels like to be loved to be held, touched, and caressed just enough
To feel needed no matter what to feel love in every touch, to feel special and that your the only one
To know and feel important to someone else
To know you have brightened somebody's day and to know they want you in everyway
And there's a passion and desire in their heart and their sure that their in love
But I wonder will I know what it feels like to be loved
I may never know

Still the girl

I'm still the girl for you I'm still the one whose true and I'm still in love with you

I never felt this love before and in my heart I feel it's you

Who can make my dreams come true if we can just start a new

It will make our relationship stronger and deeper too

If it takes us to be apart in order to be together I'm willing to

But I need to know are you still in love too and are you willing to start a new

Cause I'm still in love with you

A man

All the things it takes to be a man starts from within
Knowing rights from wrong knowing when to just listen
And knowing when to ignore your pride and just let someone in
Being patient and considered toward someone else feelings
Knowing when to say I'm sorry and when to try or give up
To follow your heart and give what's inside your soul a chance
If you're a true man you should know it's all in you

Broken wing

I am a broken wing whom promises to love and obey

But I couldn't give love because I am a broken wing

I try to fly high but I can't because I am a broken wing

I give myself physically to many but never mentally because I am a broken wing

I do many things because I can't love myself

And I make promises in the moment

Which I don't mean any of them at all cause I am a broken wing

Because of me I am broken a broken wing

All the time

Do you ever think about me do you ever remise
do you still feel the same or has time change the game
I can't believe I'm writing all of this
I should be over you but I can't time has stood still in my heart and mind
Cause I just want you all the time and to be mine
I'm sitting here thinking about the past and how it could have last
And how I could turn back the times I would have made you mine
I can't hide what I feel inside cause I think about you all the time

One

I never let you go no matter who I was with I wanted you more
I wish we could have came together as one
I'll take care of your heart and blend it with mine to be one
So you can place your heart in my hands
And I'll show you the starts and the sun
Cause I just want us to be one

Missing you

I can't stand missing you seeing your face your smile your eyes

Feeling your heart beat that should be mine

It's hard to believe your not here or near

Cause I cant stand missing you

I want to be more than just friends

So please tell me where do we go from here

I can't stop these feelings I have for you

You make me love and want you too

Lord knows why you are still on my mind

Boy it's true that I'm still in love with you

All I want is you and I don't know what to do

Cause I can't stand missing you

What you mean

I remember the day I first saw you I knew you had to be mine
As time went on we never came together
But I prayed to god that some day we will
You don't know what you mean to me
I get butterflies when I hear or see you next to me
Like the clouds to the sky I'll give you my heart and mind
I know were suppose to be friends but I do love you and care
You don't know what you mean to me

The most

Passion was in the air as if we were lovers and everybody thought we were too

We did almost everything together we talked on the phone for hours on end

You wanted me just as much as I wanted you

I didn't care about your friends I just wanted you next to me

I'm willing to tell you everything unsaid between you and me

Should I take a chance now or is it too late

Cause you're the one I want to be with the most

I see you

I see you

Just what do you see

Is it my beauty that you see in me

Is it my smile, my eyes

My cheek bones set so high

Is it my breast so big and round

Is it my flat stomach or long legs with big calf's

Is it my firm butt set high up

Or is it the hair that I brought

So please tell me what you see in me

I see the beauty deep from within

I see your soul through your eyes

I see the courage through your smile

I see a heart that's warm inside

And I see that you're a human being with courage

And knowledge to be that's what I see

Can't you see what can see

Face

It's been too long last time I saw your face

I been in love a time or two but in the end I still chose you

Do you want me anything like I want you

No one could love you the way I do

I'm sure of what I'm feeling cause my heart tells me too

Do I ever cross your mind and do you feel the same

Or has love faded away

Never told you

I never told you how much you meant to me

From first sight I knew instantly

Your part of me my soul, my heart, and my mind

I would satisfy your every need

If you would just come to me

It's hard to keep it all in when I'm around you I just want to give in

You will always be the man for me for all times

How can I

How can I be wrong when I feel the way I do
If you don't know how I feel then let me show you that I'm for real
I should be over you but that's just not the case
I hope you will see that you and I were meant to be
I get down on my knees and pray to god that we will be
These no place I would rather be
My only regret is not being with you and you with me

Scared

I'm scared of telling you how I feel that I love you

And have been in love with you for all of these years

You turned down my love once before

I don't know if I should open that door

But I do know that no one else can love you like I do

I'll be there to give advice and trust boy you know what's up

And if you're looking for some one here I am

Someone who understands who you are and what you need as a man

I'm not asking for much it's all up to you what do you want to do

For me

You're the only one for me what are your hopes and dreams

Things did not turn out the way they were suppose to be

How the days play back in my mind

I prayed so many nights for you to be mine

I don't want to hide what I feel inside

Cause I want to be your lady and feel the warmth of you next to me

For I will treasure that day for as long as I can have you next to me

Does she

Does she love you the way I do

Does she make you feel the way I use too

I wander does she make you smile

Or give advice when there's something on your mind

Does she listen to you

Does she make love the way you knew I could

Does she have your heart in your hands are you always going to be her man

Can she cook like me

Can she do the things I do or is she not like me

Does she explore like me or are you feeling her the same way you still feel me

So true

I wish I could hear from you right now
You were suppose to be here next to me
I don't know if I can ever get over you
The way I feel is so true
I'm right here with open arms just waiting for you to come through
This time I'm not letting go until you come to me
Why don't you give my love a try cause you're the man of my dreams
A love like ours don't happen everyday
So tell me will you come to me and stay

Sister

So what can you tell me about your sister

Is she kind is she giving, thoughtful, loving, loyal, respectful

Does she love you as much as you love her

Can she do all the things you need her to do

Does she just show up

Is she your best friend is she the women you wish you were

Is she there for you mentally at all

Does she just give you a hug

Does she tell you she love you

Does she call when nothing is up

Or is this the sister you always wanted

Believe

Trust and believe in the person you see

Trust in what you feel and can be

Trust in your process of being a new being

Trust and believe in yourself and what you need

Trust in yourself that you can be free

Trust what's within and you will find the key

Losing control

I want you so it's in my soul I want you so it's in my bones

I want you so I'm losing control your part of my spirit and I am yours

Don't you know I'll give all my love to you if you want me too

Can't you see all the love I have inside can't you see it through my eyes

I never loved you so much as I do today

And when I fell in love I didn't know it would be forever from that day

End of time

I have always love you but I'm scared you don't feel the same
As I do when I hear your name I have always loved you
But I'm scared if we give us a chance our friendship will not last
And that's something I can't live without till this day
God knows I have always loved you and I am your ribbon in the sky
I know our love will grow for I will be your women and you my man
Cause I will always love you till the end of time

Someone

I'm in love with someone who don't love me

I'm in love with someone who can't see me for me

I'm in love with someone who dreams isn't me

I'm in love with someone so desperately

I'm in love with you can't you see me

Our hopes and dreams our future of us just being together as one

Can't you see all the possibilities

Were already friends were as close as two people can be with out the love affair

I'm in love can't you be in love with me

Stay

If you need someone you can always count on me To fulfill your fantasy

All the secret places that's within I will uncover with the touch of your skin

So can I get to know you and explore your mind heart and soul

I can't wait to meet them all cause you're the only one for me

And I want you to stay with me

I never knew I could feel this way how it would be a dream to have you next to me

My heart will never stray sometimes I don't know what to say

Cause you're in my mind night and day

So can you please stay with me

A dream

The closer you got to me and you caressing me made my body shiver

You were holding me and I started rubbing your face

Then I rubbed your back gently

You kissed me with such ease

We started making love desperately

but I woke up cause it was just a dream

How I wish this would come true

I have all these feelings and I don't know what to do

Just need to talk to you and tell you that I'm in love with you

And I could only hope that you feel the same or take it day by day

Love affair

I never walked away I was with you in your heart and mind
I was always by your side I was the shadow when you walked
I was the tears when you cried
I was the confusion in your mind
I was the beat of your heart
I was the one who wanted you the most
The one you called on when you needed a friend I was there from within
I'm the music in the songs you sang
I am the smile on your face
I am the touch of your skin
And you are forever my love affair

next to me

What are you thinking only you know and god you know too
Can you please tell me so I can make it through all the pain
From you not being with me I tried it before and we couldn't make it through
Stay with me for the rest of our lives and I promise to love you for life
Let me know do you want me or do you wan to be just friends
Let me know if I need to control what's within
I'm going crazy cause I want you next to me

The same

When we met I knew I wanted you as time went by

I wanted you even more than I even knew

But your friends made it impossible for you to love me too

The way I wanted you too

So I got with another and I stayed with him for years

But everyday I thought about you and how I feel

every time he touched me I thought about you making love to me

You are my everything and I need you with me

I can't get you out of my mind and how I want you to be mine

Everybody's got an opinion on how they think our story is going to end

But only you and I can tell what's within

It's killing me you not being with me

Don't you know I would love you forever and a day

And I want you to do the same

Start

I know in your heart you love me too

Like night to day I want to be with you

Nothing will change the love I had inside

Cause with you I feel it's right

But I tell you everything but the truth

That I'm in love with you and I don't know what to do

I'll give you the best part of me my heart

and I promise to love you for life if we just start

Cause with you I know I can make it right

If you could just hold me through the night

Breathe

I can hardly breathe cause what you do to me

You make my heart skip a beat every time you're next to me

My body is calling out your name please tell me you feel the same

Cause I want to be with you more than you ever know

You are suppose to be here with me

I'm only thinking of you and me and what we could do together

For I prayed everyday that you would come to me forever

Cause I can't breathe without you next to me

Exhale

I want to exhale but I can't cause I don't have you next to me
I want to exhale but I can't cause your only in my dreams
My heart is crying out for you don't you hear the beat
I would love you forever and a day
I never felt this way until you came my way
I want to exhale

Killing me

I was dying inside in my spirit

I did things to kill myself slowly

I lived a lie

I just laid down to die

Doing things that wasn't for me

My spirit and health was killing me

And I was letting it do it to me

I loved but didn't choose correctly

I cried inside of me

I weep for my mental being

And I wasn't loving me

I did things to myself because I allowed it

I didn't love myself because I didn't fight it

But today I live because I take time for me wouldn't you agree

Like you

You are not alone there is always someone just like you

Either a better or worse side of you

But it's up to you to be the best you

You can be whatever that means for you

Open your heart and everything will fall in place if you let it

Lost

I was lost in something that was bigger than me

I was lost in all my fears and dreams

I didn't listen to the voice inside of me

And did something that was not meant for me

And still and all I don't regret the path I took

I just rerouted myself to get to where I'm suppose to be

And at the end of it all I found myself and the hunger I have for it all

I'm glad I took this journey at all because I got out of it what I was suppose too

And the should've could've would've is out the door

Cause I'm living my life to the fullest ad I'm just glad for it all

Life

Do you hear it but most of all did you listen

To what life is trying to tell you

But most of all God or your most high

Did you feel it the love and all that it has in store

Do you see it the beauty all around the sky the clouds

The stars the tree's the mountains the water and the human being

Do you see the beauty from within and the meaning of it all

Do you like it the person that's inside

But most of all do you love you and who you are

Can you see it I see it I can see it all

I am

I profess what I have inside all the love I gave you that was mine
The love I should've gave to myself I gave to you without a thought
And I lost myself in the process of it all
All the things that made me, me
And new I was more than what I see and felt and was being
And when I finally close that chapter of that love
I found me all of me and all that I am

Grateful

Can you be grateful for everything you have

Can you complete the task at hand

Can you just show up for yourself all the time

And can you give passion to what you are trying to find

Everyone has a gift you just have to find yours

And try your best to make the best of what you have

And all that's in store

Time

Is it really on your side cause you been wasting time

With someone whom don't love you

With someone who doesn't respect you

With someone whom said they will be loyal to you but their not

You just been wasting all this time

And you think let me just give them one more time

Let me keep trying and maybe their be mine

But you are just wasting time

You can't see what needs to be

If their not for you then it can't be

So don't waist time cause it's not on you side

Love

Love that four letter word means so much than people use it for
They use the word to loosely
But truth be told how can you love someone you don't know
How can you love someone you can't hold
Or touch or feel but truth is God is love
So you should love everything that is of him
And that's the deal of it all

The rose

The mind feeds off the earth and blossoms like a rose
Getting bigger and better, bigger than you know
Learning new and different things each and everyday
Listening and receiving every thought in everyway
Exploring and discovering every new idea
Just wanting to learn with all it's will
So take that flower and let it bloom
To become the rose that it should

Mind

If you have a mind that you want to grow feed it
With knowledge to help it grow
Nurture it with wisdom and happy thoughts
And you will find that your mind will explore

Tomorrow

When you are sad or depress just think about tomorrow
And it will ease the pain for it will bring a new day
Filled of hopes and dreams for your future ahead
Looking forward to tomorrow brings so much joy
Because you can start all over and forget about your last thought
For it will bring joy because tomorrow is a day filled with it all

Soul

Do you know what a human soul is

Obviously you don't

Because if you did you wouldn't be worried about colors at all

You wouldn't care who your son or daughter dated or who lives next door

You'll just try to find peace and happiness for all our souls

Cry

I hear the wind whispering softly
I hear the birds singing lively
I smell the roses that smell so sweet
I hear their voices crying help me
I see the hunger in their eyes
Which is not to my surprise
I feel their bones weak and frail
I feel their struggle as if I was there
I feel their pain in everyway
I pray for their souls everyday
God please take it away what the endure everyday

Mirror

Look into the mirror and tell me what you see
Is it the face that you want to be
Look into the mirror and tell me what you feel
Is it love and respect for the one who's left there
When you look into the mirror don't you hear
The voices crying help me I'm still hear
When you look into the mirror don't you
Want to find your true self so that
You can know what life is really about
Look into the mirror and you will find the key
To you being free just take a look and
You'll see the true being

Wake up

When we started out I just needed you to fill the void
that was left from my father's death
But as time went by I got closer and closer to you
I wanted you more at least I thought it was you
We had a child and I got even more attached
Everyday life was just a common act
I wanted you more but you didn't want me back
You fooled around just like that
Me being stupid I played blind
Because I didn't want to lose my love at that time
But wouldn't you believe I woke up
because I realized that it was daddy that I really wanted

Daddy loves me

I'm searching for my father where can he be

I'll never believe that daddy has left me

Oh wait here he comes daddy's back in another form

This time I'll love him more I know I'll give him unconditional love

Whatever you do it won't bother me

Because I'll always know that daddy loves me

I'll treat you the best just like a king

And I'll over look your guilty ways if you would just love me

But wait is this really daddy I don't know

But I'll wait around to see

If not it's my fault I know the deal just watch and see

But I don't care as long as I know that daddy loves me

The love game

When women and men first meet

Application process should be complete

Points and references has to be good

Because women want someone to do good by them

Taking them out and doing new and exciting things

Because property tax is part of the game

Rates go up if you don't do right

Because loans for love is just not right

Satisfaction guarantee as long as you with me you'll never need

It's a shame that men think that all women are about games

When all we really want is love ain't that a shame

Human soul

Can you guess what the color of my skin is
For I am mixed with Irish and French
Dutch and Indian, west Indian and African too
For I am a melting pot for so many races just like you
But what color am I do you know
For I have no color I'm just a human soul

What's inside of me

As I lay here I wonder how would it be

To be another race besides the one inside of me

Would they treat me different probably like a queen

But would it be worth it to change my identity just for a theme

I sit here and wonder how would I feel

Would I feel better or worse than I feel now

Will I have the same self respect as I do now

Or will I be worthless not knowing where or how

So I would rather be nothing more than the race that's inside of me

Knowing what I already know and feeling the way I do

My race is the best and you better believe that's the truth

Insane

Did you hear my heart skip a beat

Cause I'm next to you and you to me

every time the phone rings I wish it was you calling me

I promise you I'm here for you forever and a day

I never thought I could feel this way

You got me going insane for the love I know wouldn't stray

So please tell me you feel the same

Cause I just want you next to me

Empty

When I am empty I fill it with empty ness

When I am sad I fill it with sadness

When I'm broken I find someone who is more broken than me

When I need love I find someone with the promise

But not the commitment to love me

When I give love I don't give it to myself the way it needs to be

Or the way I gave I out

It's funny how you end up finding all the things

That's already in you in someone else

Love song

I love you like a love song where did we go wrong
I thought we would be together forever
But I guess I was wrong
How did we let so much time slip away
You and I were meant to be
I never got you out of my heart and mind
I think about you all the time
All the precious moments we shared it seems like yesterday
God only knows how my heart still moans for you
God knows it's true
I will always feel what we had we were lovers without the love affair
And I do love you and care
I hope you still feel like before
Cause I can't change what happened in the past
But this time I just want my fair chance
And I want it to last but only time will tell if we pick up from the past
Cause I know in my heart I'm the best for you
Won't you be that special one too

Today

What we go through is nobody's business but me and you
We struggle to stay together but truth be told
you don't want me and I don't want you
We have different agendas of what we were going to do
Yours is playing around mines is thinking about how to get
the one who never left m heart and mind
But I've learned from yesterday what to do today
Because today is a brand new day

Affairs of the Heart

We were so young when we first met
Immediately there was an attraction from you and me
I looked at you and I knew I wanted you for life
We never got together and so many years passed us by
But I never forgot that feeling how my heart felt
With every moment we spent together
Every phone call every song you sung
Every playful touch
My heart stayed frozen in time
You saved me from all the outside pain
And all the confusion in my mind
Love is such a beautiful thing and it just made me
Want you more and more each day
These are my affairs of the heart

For your eyes only

Can't you see what's right in front of thee

When I gave you the twelve days of Christmas

I gave from my heart cause I love you can't you see

The things we did we were always suppose to be together

All the laughing and joking

All the secrets being told

All the nights on the phone

ALL the time we spent together is in my heart for good it's like solid gold

Sitting at the piano you singing songs

Singing a ribbon in the sky was my favorite song

Will I'll story end like a fairy tale

Or will I be heartbroken like before

Only time will tell

Printed in the United States
By Bookmasters